Barbecue notes and perfected recipes

BY: ROB AINBINDER
DESIGN & LAYOUT BY: MICHAEL HALL

© Copyright 2018 Pitmaster's Log Book / barbecuelogbook.com

TABLE OF CONTENTS

Acknowledgement 3
About Rob Ainbinder 3
About Pitmaster's Barbecue Log Book 4
Why a Barbecue Log Book? 4
Beef Cuts Illustration 5
Pork Cuts Illustration 5
Wood Smoking Chart 6
Using the Barbecue Log Book 7
Sections of Barbecue Log Book page 7

ACKNOWLEDGEMENT

The Pitmaster's Barbecue Log Book is dedicated to my wife, Angela. She was the single reason I learned anything about Texas barbecue and ignited a passion for barbecue in me. Her unending love and support are what made this possible. Love you.

Others that I must thank include my friend Michael Hall for his help in layout and guiding the branding of the Barbecue Log Book and Lucas Alcalde of Kegs & Code for sharing his experiences with me and tons of encouragement to make this project happen.

ABOUT ROB AINBINDER

Rob Ainbinder is a husband to his wife Angela and a father to his daughter, Natalie. Rob has been an online marketer for more than 15 years and has pursued his passion for barbecue for an equal amount of time. To connect with Rob, visit www.robainbinder.com.

ABOUT PITMASTER'S BARBECUE LOG BOOK

The Barbecue Log Book is for the aspiring and the accomplished pitmaster. Whether you are experimenting with smoking on a grill or, have moved on to an offset pit, or a pellet smoker this logbook will help you build an understanding around what works and what doesn't. It doesn't matter if you just took your new smoker out of the box or, have been cooking for a decade with a pit thermometer, remote thermometer or, WiFi data logger... Pitmaster's Barbecue Log Book will become a permanent record and indispensable reference in your quest for the ultimate barbecue. It is also a family record of the many gatherings and celebrations ou helped to bring to life. Finally, the Barbecue Log Book is a family heirloom, of sorts. You can share your success and learnings with future generations of barbecue pitmasters in your family.

WHY A BARBECUE LOG BOOK?

I developed the Barbecue Log Book after writing down the progress of my cooks on various paper pads and pieces of college ruled filler paper. These pieces of paper became tattered over time risking the loss of information. I wanted something better, more concise and more permanent than what I was using. And the Pitmaster's Barbecue Log Book is my answer to that challenge.

BEEF CUTS ILLUSTRATION

PORK CUTS ILLUSTRATION

WOOD SMOKING CHART

	BEEF	PORK	POULTRY	SEAFOOD	LAMB	VEGGIES	CHEESE
ALDER		🔥	🔥	🔥			
APPLE			🔥	🔥	🔥		
CHERRY	🔥	🔥	🔥	🔥	🔥		
HICKORY	🔥	🔥					🔥
MAPLE			🔥			🔥	
MESQUITE	🔥	🔥					🔥
MULBERRY		🔥	🔥	🔥			
OAK	🔥	🔥	🔥	🔥	🔥		
OLIVE			🔥				
PEACH		🔥	🔥				
PEAR		🔥	🔥				
PECAN	🔥	🔥	🔥				
WALNUT	🔥	🔥					

USING THE BARBECUE LOG BOOK

Each part of a page has a specific use and using it regularly will help you learn about the specifics of cooking with your barbeque pit regardless of weather, wind, or amount of food you are cooking.

SECTIONS OF BARBECUE LOG BOOK PAGE

Date: Enter the day of the cook.

Weather: Fill in sunrise & set times as well as high, low temperature and humidity

Wind: Indicate direction and speed of wind.

Menu/Purpose: If you know what else will be served add it in here. Fill in your reason for the cook.

Rub/Sauce Used: Enter the page/name/brand of the rub/sauce used.

Time: Current time

Temp: Outside air temperature

Pit Temp: Temperature of the cooking chamber, usually measured at grate level

Meat: Internal temperature of meat

Fuel/Notes: Add notes on changes to dampeners, amount of wood/charcoal added, etc.

DATE/S: _____

WEATHER

High: Sunrise:
Low: Sunset:
Humidity:

WIND

Wind Speed:
Wind Direction:

MENU/PURPOSE:

RUB & SAUCE USED:

TIME	AIR TEMP	PIT TEMP	MEAT TEMP	FUEL & NOTES

DATE/S: _____

WEATHER

High:
Low:
Humidity:

Sunrise:
Sunset:

WIND

Wind Speed:
Wind Direction:

MENU/PURPOSE:

RUB & SAUCE USED:

TIME	AIR TEMP	PIT TEMP	MEAT TEMP	FUEL & NOTES

DATE/S: _____

WEATHER

High: Sunrise:
Low: Sunset:
Humidity:

WIND

Wind Speed:
Wind Direction:

MENU/PURPOSE:

RUB & SAUCE USED:

TIME	AIR TEMP	PIT TEMP	MEAT TEMP	FUEL & NOTES

DATE/S: _____

WEATHER

High: ____ Sunrise: ____
Low: ____ Sunset: ____
Humidity: ____

WIND

Wind Speed: ____
Wind Direction: ____

MENU/PURPOSE:

_____

_____

RUB & SAUCE USED:

_____

TIME	AIR TEMP	PIT TEMP	MEAT TEMP	FUEL & NOTES

DATE/S: _____

WEATHER

High: Sunrise:
Low: Sunset:
Humidity:

WIND

Wind Speed:
Wind Direction:

MENU/PURPOSE:

RUB & SAUCE USED:

TIME	AIR TEMP	PIT TEMP	MEAT TEMP	FUEL & NOTES

DATE/S: _____

WEATHER

High: Sunrise:
Low: Sunset:
Humidity:

WIND

Wind Speed:
Wind Direction:

MENU/PURPOSE:

RUB & SAUCE USED:

TIME	AIR TEMP	PIT TEMP	MEAT TEMP	FUEL & NOTES

DATE/S: _____

WEATHER

High: Sunrise:
Low: Sunset:
Humidity:

WIND

Wind Speed:
Wind Direction:

MENU/PURPOSE:

RUB & SAUCE USED:

TIME	AIR TEMP	PIT TEMP	MEAT TEMP	FUEL & NOTES

DATE/S: _____

WEATHER

High: Sunrise:
Low: Sunset:
Humidity:

WIND

Wind Speed:
Wind Direction:

MENU/PURPOSE:

_____

RUB & SAUCE USED:

_____

TIME	AIR TEMP	PIT TEMP	MEAT TEMP	FUEL & NOTES

DATE/S: _____

WEATHER

High: Sunrise:
Low: Sunset:
Humidity:

WIND

Wind Speed:
Wind Direction:

MENU/PURPOSE:

RUB & SAUCE USED:

TIME	AIR TEMP	PIT TEMP	MEAT TEMP	FUEL & NOTES

DATE/S: _____

WEATHER

High: Sunrise:
Low: Sunset:
Humidity:

WIND

Wind Speed:
Wind Direction:

MENU/PURPOSE:

RUB & SAUCE USED:

TIME	AIR TEMP	PIT TEMP	MEAT TEMP	FUEL & NOTES

DATE/S: _____

WEATHER

High: Sunrise:
Low: Sunset:
Humidity:

WIND

Wind Speed:
Wind Direction:

MENU/PURPOSE:

RUB & SAUCE USED:

TIME	AIR TEMP	PIT TEMP	MEAT TEMP	FUEL & NOTES

DATE/S: _____

WEATHER

High: Sunrise:
Low: Sunset:
Humidity:

WIND

Wind Speed:
Wind Direction:

MENU/PURPOSE:

_____

RUB & SAUCE USED:

_____

TIME	AIR TEMP	PIT TEMP	MEAT TEMP	FUEL & NOTES

DATE/S: _____

WEATHER

High: Sunrise:
Low: Sunset:
Humidity:

WIND

Wind Speed:
Wind Direction:

MENU/PURPOSE:

RUB & SAUCE USED:

TIME	AIR TEMP	PIT TEMP	MEAT TEMP	FUEL & NOTES

DATE/S: _____

WEATHER

High: Sunrise:
Low: Sunset:
Humidity:

WIND

Wind Speed:
Wind Direction:

MENU/PURPOSE:

RUB & SAUCE USED:

TIME	AIR TEMP	PIT TEMP	MEAT TEMP	FUEL & NOTES

DATE/S: _____

WEATHER

High:
Low:
Humidity:

Sunrise:
Sunset:

WIND

Wind Speed:
Wind Direction:

MENU/PURPOSE:

RUB & SAUCE USED:

TIME	AIR TEMP	PIT TEMP	MEAT TEMP	FUEL & NOTES

DATE/S: _____

WEATHER

High: Sunrise:
Low: Sunset:
Humidity:

WIND

Wind Speed:
Wind Direction:

MENU/PURPOSE:

_____

_____

RUB & SAUCE USED:

_____

TIME	AIR TEMP	PIT TEMP	MEAT TEMP	FUEL & NOTES

DATE/S: _____

WEATHER

High:　　　Sunrise:
Low:　　　 Sunset:
Humidity:

WIND

Wind Speed:

Wind Direction:

MENU/PURPOSE:

RUB & SAUCE USED:

TIME	AIR TEMP	PIT TEMP	MEAT TEMP	FUEL & NOTES

DATE/S: _____

WEATHER

High: Sunrise:
Low: Sunset:
Humidity:

WIND

Wind Speed:
Wind Direction:

MENU/PURPOSE:

_____

RUB & SAUCE USED:

_____

TIME	AIR TEMP	PIT TEMP	MEAT TEMP	FUEL & NOTES

DATE/S: _____

WEATHER

High: Sunrise:
Low: Sunset:
Humidity:

WIND

Wind Speed:
Wind Direction:

MENU/PURPOSE:

RUB & SAUCE USED:

TIME	AIR TEMP	PIT TEMP	MEAT TEMP	FUEL & NOTES

DATE/S: _____

WEATHER

High: Sunrise:

Low: Sunset:

Humidity:

WIND

Wind Speed:

Wind Direction:

MENU/PURPOSE:

_____

RUB & SAUCE USED:

_____

TIME	AIR TEMP	PIT TEMP	MEAT TEMP	FUEL & NOTES

DATE/S: _____

WEATHER

High: Sunrise:
Low: Sunset:
Humidity:

WIND

Wind Speed:
Wind Direction:

MENU/PURPOSE:

_____

RUB & SAUCE USED:

_____

TIME	AIR TEMP	PIT TEMP	MEAT TEMP	FUEL & NOTES

DATE/S: _____

WEATHER

High: Sunrise:
Low: Sunset:
Humidity:

WIND

Wind Speed:
Wind Direction:

MENU/PURPOSE:

RUB & SAUCE USED:

TIME	AIR TEMP	PIT TEMP	MEAT TEMP	FUEL & NOTES

DATE/S: _____

WEATHER

High:　　　Sunrise:
Low:　　　 Sunset:
Humidity:

WIND

Wind Speed:

Wind Direction:

MENU/PURPOSE:

RUB & SAUCE USED:

TIME	AIR TEMP	PIT TEMP	MEAT TEMP	FUEL & NOTES

DATE/S: _____

WEATHER

High: Sunrise:
Low: Sunset:
Humidity:

WIND

Wind Speed:
Wind Direction:

MENU/PURPOSE:

_____

_____

RUB & SAUCE USED:

_____

TIME	AIR TEMP	PIT TEMP	MEAT TEMP	FUEL & NOTES

DATE/S: _____

WEATHER

High: Sunrise:
Low: Sunset:
Humidity:

WIND

Wind Speed:
Wind Direction:

MENU/PURPOSE:

RUB & SAUCE USED:

TIME	AIR TEMP	PIT TEMP	MEAT TEMP	FUEL & NOTES

DATE/S: _____

WEATHER

High: Sunrise:
Low: Sunset:
Humidity:

WIND

Wind Speed:
Wind Direction:

MENU/PURPOSE:

RUB & SAUCE USED:

TIME	AIR TEMP	PIT TEMP	MEAT TEMP	FUEL & NOTES

DATE/S: _____

WEATHER

High:
Low:
Humidity:

Sunrise:
Sunset:

WIND

Wind Speed:
Wind Direction:

MENU/PURPOSE:

TIME	AIR TEMP	PIT TEMP	MEAT TEMP	FUEL & NOTES

RUB & SAUCE USED:

DATE/S: _____

WEATHER

High:
Low:
Humidity:

Sunrise:
Sunset:

WIND

Wind Speed:
Wind Direction:

MENU/PURPOSE:

RUB & SAUCE USED:

TIME	AIR TEMP	PIT TEMP	MEAT TEMP	FUEL & NOTES

DATE/S: _____

WEATHER

High: Sunrise:
Low: Sunset:
Humidity:

WIND

Wind Speed:
Wind Direction:

MENU/PURPOSE:

RUB & SAUCE USED:

TIME	AIR TEMP	PIT TEMP	MEAT TEMP	FUEL & NOTES

DATE/S: _____

WEATHER

High: Sunrise:
Low: Sunset:
Humidity:

WIND

Wind Speed:

Wind Direction:

MENU/PURPOSE:

_____

RUB & SAUCE USED:

_____

TIME	AIR TEMP	PIT TEMP	MEAT TEMP	FUEL & NOTES

DATE/S: _____

WEATHER   **WIND**

High: _____   Sunrise: _____   Wind Speed: _____

Low: _____   Sunset: _____   Wind Direction: _____

Humidity: _____

MENU/PURPOSE:

RUB & SAUCE USED:

TIME	AIR TEMP	PIT TEMP	MEAT TEMP	FUEL & NOTES

DATE/S: _____

WEATHER

High: Sunrise:
Low: Sunset:
Humidity:

WIND

Wind Speed:

Wind Direction:

MENU/PURPOSE:

RUB & SAUCE USED:

TIME	AIR TEMP	PIT TEMP	MEAT TEMP	FUEL & NOTES

DATE/S: _____

WEATHER

High: Sunrise:
Low: Sunset:
Humidity:

WIND

Wind Speed:
Wind Direction:

MENU/PURPOSE:

RUB & SAUCE USED:

TIME	AIR TEMP	PIT TEMP	MEAT TEMP	FUEL & NOTES

DATE/S: _____

WEATHER

High: Sunrise:
Low: Sunset:
Humidity:

WIND

Wind Speed:
Wind Direction:

MENU/PURPOSE:

RUB & SAUCE USED:

TIME	AIR TEMP	PIT TEMP	MEAT TEMP	FUEL & NOTES

DATE/S: _____

WEATHER

High: Sunrise:

Low: Sunset:

Humidity:

WIND

Wind Speed:

Wind Direction:

MENU/PURPOSE:

RUB & SAUCE USED:

TIME	AIR TEMP	PIT TEMP	MEAT TEMP	FUEL & NOTES

DATE/S: _____

WEATHER

High: Sunrise:
Low: Sunset:
Humidity:

WIND

Wind Speed:

Wind Direction:

MENU/PURPOSE:

RUB & SAUCE USED:

TIME	AIR TEMP	PIT TEMP	MEAT TEMP	FUEL & NOTES

DATE/S: _____

WEATHER

High: Sunrise:

Low: Sunset:

Humidity:

WIND

Wind Speed:

Wind Direction:

MENU/PURPOSE:

RUB & SAUCE USED:

TIME	AIR TEMP	PIT TEMP	MEAT TEMP	FUEL & NOTES

DATE/S: _____

WEATHER

High: Sunrise:
Low: Sunset:
Humidity:

WIND

Wind Speed:
Wind Direction:

MENU/PURPOSE:

_____

_____

RUB & SAUCE USED:

_____

TIME	AIR TEMP	PIT TEMP	MEAT TEMP	FUEL & NOTES

DATE/S: _____

WEATHER
High:
Low:
Humidity:

Sunrise:
Sunset:

WIND
Wind Speed:
Wind Direction:

MENU/PURPOSE:

RUB & SAUCE USED:

TIME	AIR TEMP	PIT TEMP	MEAT TEMP	FUEL & NOTES

DATE/S: _____

WEATHER

High: Sunrise:
Low: Sunset:
Humidity:

WIND

Wind Speed:
Wind Direction:

MENU/PURPOSE:

RUB & SAUCE USED:

TIME	AIR TEMP	PIT TEMP	MEAT TEMP	FUEL & NOTES

DATE/S: _____

WEATHER

High: Sunrise:
Low: Sunset:
Humidity:

WIND

Wind Speed:
Wind Direction:

MENU/PURPOSE:

RUB & SAUCE USED:

TIME	AIR TEMP	PIT TEMP	MEAT TEMP	FUEL & NOTES

DATE/S: _____

WEATHER

High: Sunrise:
Low: Sunset:
Humidity:

WIND

Wind Speed:
Wind Direction:

MENU/PURPOSE:

RUB & SAUCE USED:

TIME	AIR TEMP	PIT TEMP	MEAT TEMP	FUEL & NOTES

DATE/S: _____

WEATHER

High:
Low:
Humidity:

Sunrise:
Sunset:

WIND

Wind Speed:
Wind Direction:

MENU/PURPOSE:

RUB & SAUCE USED:

TIME	AIR TEMP	PIT TEMP	MEAT TEMP	FUEL & NOTES

DATE/S: _____

WEATHER

High: Sunrise:
Low: Sunset:
Humidity:

WIND

Wind Speed:
Wind Direction:

MENU/PURPOSE:

RUB & SAUCE USED:

TIME	AIR TEMP	PIT TEMP	MEAT TEMP	FUEL & NOTES

DATE/S: _____

WEATHER

High: Sunrise:
Low: Sunset:
Humidity:

WIND

Wind Speed:

Wind Direction:

MENU/PURPOSE:

RUB & SAUCE USED:

TIME	AIR TEMP	PIT TEMP	MEAT TEMP	FUEL & NOTES

DATE/S: _____

WEATHER

High: Sunrise:
Low: Sunset:
Humidity:

WIND

Wind Speed:
Wind Direction:

MENU/PURPOSE:

RUB & SAUCE USED:

TIME	AIR TEMP	PIT TEMP	MEAT TEMP	FUEL & NOTES

DATE/S: _____

WEATHER

High: Sunrise:
Low: Sunset:
Humidity:

WIND

Wind Speed:
Wind Direction:

MENU/PURPOSE:

RUB & SAUCE USED:

TIME	AIR TEMP	PIT TEMP	MEAT TEMP	FUEL & NOTES

DATE/S: _____

WEATHER

High: Sunrise:
Low: Sunset:
Humidity:

WIND

Wind Speed:
Wind Direction:

MENU/PURPOSE:

RUB & SAUCE USED:

TIME	AIR TEMP	PIT TEMP	MEAT TEMP	FUEL & NOTES

DATE/S: _____

WEATHER

High: Sunrise:

Low: Sunset:

Humidity:

WIND

Wind Speed:

Wind Direction:

MENU/PURPOSE:

RUB & SAUCE USED:

TIME	AIR TEMP	PIT TEMP	MEAT TEMP	FUEL & NOTES

DATE/S: _____

WEATHER

High: Sunrise:
Low: Sunset:
Humidity:

WIND

Wind Speed:
Wind Direction:

MENU/PURPOSE:

RUB & SAUCE USED:

TIME	AIR TEMP	PIT TEMP	MEAT TEMP	FUEL & NOTES

DATE/S: _____

WEATHER

High: Sunrise:
Low: Sunset:
Humidity:

WIND

Wind Speed:

Wind Direction:

MENU/PURPOSE:

RUB & SAUCE USED:

TIME	AIR TEMP	PIT TEMP	MEAT TEMP	FUEL & NOTES

DATE/S: _____

WEATHER

High:
Low:
Humidity:

Sunrise:
Sunset:

WIND

Wind Speed:
Wind Direction:

MENU/PURPOSE:

RUB & SAUCE USED:

TIME	AIR TEMP	PIT TEMP	MEAT TEMP	FUEL & NOTES

DATE/S: _____

WEATHER

High:
Low:
Humidity:

Sunrise:
Sunset:

WIND

Wind Speed:

Wind Direction:

MENU/PURPOSE:

RUB & SAUCE USED:

TIME	AIR TEMP	PIT TEMP	MEAT TEMP	FUEL & NOTES

DATE/S: _____

WEATHER

High: Sunrise:
Low: Sunset:
Humidity:

WIND

Wind Speed:
Wind Direction:

MENU/PURPOSE:

RUB & SAUCE USED:

TIME	AIR TEMP	PIT TEMP	MEAT TEMP	FUEL & NOTES

DATE/S: _____

WEATHER

High: Sunrise:
Low: Sunset:
Humidity:

WIND

Wind Speed:
Wind Direction:

MENU/PURPOSE:

RUB & SAUCE USED:

TIME	AIR TEMP	PIT TEMP	MEAT TEMP	FUEL & NOTES

DATE/S: _____

WEATHER

High:　　　　Sunrise:
Low:　　　　 Sunset:
Humidity:

WIND

Wind Speed:
Wind Direction:

MENU/PURPOSE:

RUB & SAUCE USED:

TIME	AIR TEMP	PIT TEMP	MEAT TEMP	FUEL & NOTES

DATE/S: _____

WEATHER

High: Sunrise:
Low: Sunset:
Humidity:

WIND

Wind Speed:
Wind Direction:

MENU/PURPOSE:

RUB & SAUCE USED:

TIME	AIR TEMP	PIT TEMP	MEAT TEMP	FUEL & NOTES

DATE/S: _____

WEATHER

High: Sunrise:
Low: Sunset:
Humidity:

WIND

Wind Speed:
Wind Direction:

MENU/PURPOSE:

RUB & SAUCE USED:

TIME	AIR TEMP	PIT TEMP	MEAT TEMP	FUEL & NOTES

DATE/S: _____

WEATHER

High: Sunrise:
Low: Sunset:
Humidity:

WIND

Wind Speed:
Wind Direction:

MENU/PURPOSE:

RUB & SAUCE USED:

TIME	AIR TEMP	PIT TEMP	MEAT TEMP	FUEL & NOTES

DATE/S: _____

WEATHER

High: Sunrise:
Low: Sunset:
Humidity:

WIND

Wind Speed:
Wind Direction:

MENU/PURPOSE:

RUB & SAUCE USED:

TIME	AIR TEMP	PIT TEMP	MEAT TEMP	FUEL & NOTES

DATE/S: _____

WEATHER

High: Sunrise:
Low: Sunset:
Humidity:

WIND

Wind Speed:
Wind Direction:

MENU/PURPOSE:

RUB & SAUCE USED:

TIME	AIR TEMP	PIT TEMP	MEAT TEMP	FUEL & NOTES

DATE/S: _____

WEATHER

High: Sunrise:
Low: Sunset:
Humidity:

WIND

Wind Speed:
Wind Direction:

MENU/PURPOSE:

RUB & SAUCE USED:

TIME	AIR TEMP	PIT TEMP	MEAT TEMP	FUEL & NOTES

DATE/S: _____

WEATHER

High: Sunrise:
Low: Sunset:
Humidity:

WIND

Wind Speed:
Wind Direction:

MENU/PURPOSE:

RUB & SAUCE USED:

TIME	AIR TEMP	PIT TEMP	MEAT TEMP	FUEL & NOTES

DATE/S: _____

WEATHER

High:
Low:
Humidity:

Sunrise:
Sunset:

WIND

Wind Speed:
Wind Direction:

MENU/PURPOSE:

RUB & SAUCE USED:

TIME	AIR TEMP	PIT TEMP	MEAT TEMP	FUEL & NOTES

DATE/S: _____

WEATHER

High: Sunrise:
Low: Sunset:
Humidity:

WIND

Wind Speed:
Wind Direction:

MENU/PURPOSE:

RUB & SAUCE USED:

TIME	AIR TEMP	PIT TEMP	MEAT TEMP	FUEL & NOTES

DATE/S: _____

WEATHER

High: Sunrise:
Low: Sunset:
Humidity:

WIND

Wind Speed:
Wind Direction:

MENU/PURPOSE:

RUB & SAUCE USED:

TIME	AIR TEMP	PIT TEMP	MEAT TEMP	FUEL & NOTES

DATE/S: _____

WEATHER

High: Sunrise:
Low: Sunset:
Humidity:

WIND

Wind Speed:
Wind Direction:

MENU/PURPOSE:

RUB & SAUCE USED:

TIME	AIR TEMP	PIT TEMP	MEAT TEMP	FUEL & NOTES

DATE/S: _____

WEATHER

High:
Low:
Humidity:

Sunrise:
Sunset:

WIND

Wind Speed:
Wind Direction:

MENU/PURPOSE:

RUB & SAUCE USED:

TIME	AIR TEMP	PIT TEMP	MEAT TEMP	FUEL & NOTES

DATE/S: _____

WEATHER

High: Sunrise:
Low: Sunset:
Humidity:

WIND

Wind Speed:
Wind Direction:

MENU/PURPOSE:

RUB & SAUCE USED:

TIME	AIR TEMP	PIT TEMP	MEAT TEMP	FUEL & NOTES

DATE/S: _____

WEATHER

High: Sunrise:
Low: Sunset:
Humidity:

WIND

Wind Speed:
Wind Direction:

MENU/PURPOSE:

RUB & SAUCE USED:

TIME	AIR TEMP	PIT TEMP	MEAT TEMP	FUEL & NOTES

DATE/S: _____

WEATHER

High: _____   Sunrise: _____
Low: _____   Sunset: _____
Humidity: _____

WIND

Wind Speed: _____
Wind Direction: _____

MENU/PURPOSE: _____

RUB & SAUCE USED:

TIME	AIR TEMP	PIT TEMP	MEAT TEMP	FUEL & NOTES

DATE/S: _____

WEATHER

High: Sunrise:
Low: Sunset:
Humidity:

WIND

Wind Speed:
Wind Direction:

MENU/PURPOSE:

RUB & SAUCE USED:

TIME	AIR TEMP	PIT TEMP	MEAT TEMP	FUEL & NOTES

DATE/S: _____

WEATHER

High: Sunrise:
Low: Sunset:
Humidity:

WIND

Wind Speed:
Wind Direction:

MENU/PURPOSE:

RUB & SAUCE USED:

TIME	AIR TEMP	PIT TEMP	MEAT TEMP	FUEL & NOTES

DATE/S: _____

WEATHER

High: _____   Sunrise: _____
Low: _____   Sunset: _____
Humidity: _____

WIND

Wind Speed: _____
Wind Direction: _____

MENU/PURPOSE: _____

RUB & SAUCE USED: _____

TIME	AIR TEMP	PIT TEMP	MEAT TEMP	FUEL & NOTES

DATE/S: _____

WEATHER

High: Sunrise:
Low: Sunset:
Humidity:

WIND

Wind Speed:
Wind Direction:

MENU/PURPOSE:

RUB & SAUCE USED:

TIME	AIR TEMP	PIT TEMP	MEAT TEMP	FUEL & NOTES

DATE/S: _____

WEATHER
High: Sunrise:
Low: Sunset:
Humidity:

WIND
Wind Speed:
Wind Direction:

MENU/PURPOSE:

RUB & SAUCE USED:

TIME	AIR TEMP	PIT TEMP	MEAT TEMP	FUEL & NOTES

DATE/S: _____

WEATHER

High: Sunrise:
Low: Sunset:
Humidity:

WIND

Wind Speed:
Wind Direction:

MENU/PURPOSE:

RUB & SAUCE USED:

TIME	AIR TEMP	PIT TEMP	MEAT TEMP	FUEL & NOTES

DATE/S: _____

WEATHER

High: Sunrise:
Low: Sunset:
Humidity:

WIND

Wind Speed:
Wind Direction:

MENU/PURPOSE:

RUB & SAUCE USED:

TIME	AIR TEMP	PIT TEMP	MEAT TEMP	FUEL & NOTES

DATE/S: _____

WEATHER

High: Sunrise:
Low: Sunset:
Humidity:

WIND

Wind Speed:
Wind Direction:

MENU/PURPOSE:

RUB & SAUCE USED:

TIME	AIR TEMP	PIT TEMP	MEAT TEMP	FUEL & NOTES

DATE/S: _____

WEATHER

High: Sunrise:

Low: Sunset:

Humidity:

WIND

Wind Speed:

Wind Direction:

MENU/PURPOSE:

RUB & SAUCE USED:

TIME	AIR TEMP	PIT TEMP	MEAT TEMP	FUEL & NOTES

DATE/S: _____

WEATHER

High: Sunrise:
Low: Sunset:
Humidity:

WIND

Wind Speed:
Wind Direction:

MENU/PURPOSE:

RUB & SAUCE USED:

TIME	AIR TEMP	PIT TEMP	MEAT TEMP	FUEL & NOTES

DATE/S: _____

WEATHER

High: Sunrise:
Low: Sunset:
Humidity:

WIND

Wind Speed:
Wind Direction:

MENU/PURPOSE:

RUB & SAUCE USED:

TIME	AIR TEMP	PIT TEMP	MEAT TEMP	FUEL & NOTES

DATE/S: _____

WEATHER

High: Sunrise:
Low: Sunset:
Humidity:

WIND

Wind Speed:
Wind Direction:

MENU/PURPOSE:

RUB & SAUCE USED:

TIME	AIR TEMP	PIT TEMP	MEAT TEMP	FUEL & NOTES

DATE/S: _____

WEATHER

High:　　　　Sunrise:
Low:　　　　 Sunset:
Humidity:

WIND

Wind Speed:
Wind Direction:

MENU/PURPOSE:

___

RUB & SAUCE USED:

___

TIME	AIR TEMP	PIT TEMP	MEAT TEMP	FUEL & NOTES

DATE/S: _____

WEATHER

High: Sunrise:
Low: Sunset:
Humidity:

WIND

Wind Speed:
Wind Direction:

MENU/PURPOSE:

RUB & SAUCE USED:

TIME	AIR TEMP	PIT TEMP	MEAT TEMP	FUEL & NOTES

DATE/S: _____

WEATHER

High: Sunrise:
Low: Sunset:
Humidity:

WIND

Wind Speed:
Wind Direction:

MENU/PURPOSE:

RUB & SAUCE USED:

TIME	AIR TEMP	PIT TEMP	MEAT TEMP	FUEL & NOTES

DATE/S: _____

WEATHER

High: Sunrise:

Low: Sunset:

Humidity:

WIND

Wind Speed:

Wind Direction:

MENU/PURPOSE:

RUB & SAUCE USED:

TIME	AIR TEMP	PIT TEMP	MEAT TEMP	FUEL & NOTES

DATE/S: _____

WEATHER

High: Sunrise:

Low: Sunset:

Humidity:

WIND

Wind Speed:

Wind Direction:

MENU/PURPOSE:

RUB & SAUCE USED:

TIME	AIR TEMP	PIT TEMP	MEAT TEMP	FUEL & NOTES

DATE/S: _____

WEATHER

High: Sunrise:
Low: Sunset:
Humidity:

WIND

Wind Speed:
Wind Direction:

MENU/PURPOSE:

RUB & SAUCE USED:

TIME	AIR TEMP	PIT TEMP	MEAT TEMP	FUEL & NOTES

DATE/S: _____

WEATHER

High: Sunrise:
Low: Sunset:
Humidity:

WIND

Wind Speed:
Wind Direction:

MENU/PURPOSE:

RUB & SAUCE USED:

TIME	AIR TEMP	PIT TEMP	MEAT TEMP	FUEL & NOTES

DATE/S: _____

WEATHER

High: Sunrise:

Low: Sunset:

Humidity:

WIND

Wind Speed:

Wind Direction:

MENU/PURPOSE:

RUB & SAUCE USED:

TIME	AIR TEMP	PIT TEMP	MEAT TEMP	FUEL & NOTES

DATE/S: _____

WEATHER

High: Sunrise:
Low: Sunset:
Humidity:

WIND

Wind Speed:
Wind Direction:

MENU/PURPOSE:

RUB & SAUCE USED:

TIME	AIR TEMP	PIT TEMP	MEAT TEMP	FUEL & NOTES

DATE/S: _____

WEATHER

High: Sunrise:
Low: Sunset:
Humidity:

WIND

Wind Speed:
Wind Direction:

MENU/PURPOSE:

RUB & SAUCE USED:

TIME	AIR TEMP	PIT TEMP	MEAT TEMP	FUEL & NOTES

Made in United States
Orlando, FL
09 March 2023